iMath
Readers

Save Now, Buy Later:
Finding Unit Prices

by Renata Brunner-Jass

Content Consultant
David T. Hughes
Mathematics Curriculum Specialist

NORWOOD HOUSE PRESS
Chicago, IL

Norwood House Press
PO Box 316598
Chicago, IL 60631

For information regarding Norwood House Press, please visit our website at
www.norwoodhousepress.com or call 866-565-2900.

Special thanks to: Heidi Doyle
Production Management: Six Red Marbles
Editors: Linda Bullock and Kendra Muntz
Printed in Heshan City, Guangdong, China. 208N—012013

Library of Congress Cataloging–in-Publication Data

Brunner-Jass, Renata.

  Save now, buy later : finding unit prices/by Renata Brunner-Jass ; content
  consultant David Hughes, mathematics curriculum specialist.
  pages cm.—(iMath)

  Audience: 10-12
  Audience: Grade 4 to 6

  Summary: "The mathematical concepts of division, multiplication, and
  decimals are introduced as a family makes plans to save money to purchase a
  new computer. Readers learn about ratios, unit prices, and price comparisons.
  Includes a discover activity, history connection, and mathematical vocabulary
  introduction"—Provided by publisher.

Includes bibliographical references and index.

ISBN 978-1-59953-569-2 (library edition : alk. paper)
ISBN 978-1-60357-538-6 (ebook)

1. Division—Juvenile literature. 2. Multiplication—Juvenile literature. I. Title.

QA115.B865 2013
513.2'13—dc23
2012024159

CONTENTS

Note to Caregivers:

Throughout this book, many questions are posed to the reader. Some are open-ended and ask what the reader thinks. Discuss these questions with your child and guide him or her in thinking through the possible answers and outcomes. There are also questions posed which have a specific answer. Encourage your child to read through the text to determine the correct answer. Most importantly, encourage answers grounded in reality while also allowing imaginations to soar. Information to help support you as you share the book with your child is provided in the back in the **Additional Notes** section.

Bold words are defined in the glossary in the back of the book.

The Saving Idea

It all started with a question. I asked Dad if I could use his computer to read my school's online newsletter. Soon after, Dad asked for a family meeting.

Grandpa, Mom, Dad, Marty, and I all share the same computer. Mom uses her work computer during the day, but sometimes she needs one in the evening, too. Dad works from home, so he uses the computer day and night.

"We need a second computer," he began. "But to do that, we are going to have to work together to find ways to save money." We agreed. And that's when the real work began.

"I'll start taking my lunch to work more often," Mom began.

"We hardly watch TV," said Marty, my sister. "Why don't we cancel cable TV?"

Grandpa nodded his head in agreement. Then, he added, "We can't cancel eating, so I say we find ways to save money on groceries."

So, we made a supermarket list. How could we buy our favorite items more cheaply? Should we buy in bulk? That would mean buying large quantities of the same product at one time. Who knew that buying more could save you money?

What's a Unit Price?

If my family is going to begin saving money on groceries, we're going to have to make some comparisons. The first step is to find the **unit price**, or the **rate**, for the items we buy most often. Units are specific measurements, such as pounds and ounces.

Recently, we bought two pounds of apples for $3.50. I can write this price as a **ratio**: $3.50 : 2 pounds.

A **ratio** compares two amounts. The ratio $3.50 : 2 compares dollars to pounds.

But how much did we pay *per pound*? That is, what unit price did we pay?

I can divide the dollar amount by the unit amount to find the unit price. And there are different **strategies** I can use to divide.

Idea 1: I can use **hundred grids** to divide. A hundred grid is a 10 × 10 square made of rows and columns. There are 100 small squares within a hundred grid.

I start by drawing three hundred grids, one for each whole dollar. Then, I draw a fourth grid for the cents. I shade 3 wholes and 50 hundredths.

We bought two pounds of apples. To find the cost per pound, I group the shaded units into two equal groups. In this case, there are no shaded units left over. So, I don't have to **round** my answer to the nearest cent to find a unit price.

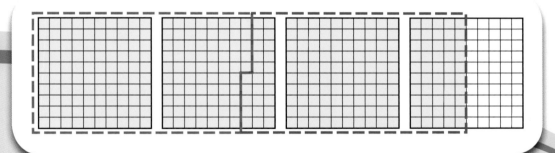

What is the unit price for a pound of apples? Can you think of other ways to divide the grids to get the same answer?

Is modeling with hundred grids a useful way to divide a **decimal number** to get a unit price? Why or why not?

Idea 2: I can make a **double number line diagram** and then use repeated subtraction to find the answer.

The number line on top represents $3.50. I label **intervals** of 25¢, from $0.00 to $3.50.

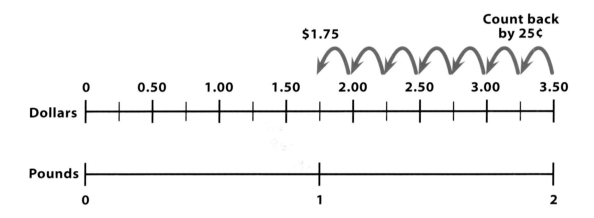

The number line on bottom is the same length. It represents 2 pounds of apples. I label intervals of 1.

Now, I subtract by $0.25 until the interval on the top number line lines up with the interval on the bottom number line. What is the unit price for a pound of apples?

Is a double number line diagram a useful model for finding a unit price? Why or why not?

Idea 3: A standard step-by-step method for solving a problem is called an **algorithm**. I can use an algorithm to find the unit price.

I think of this problem-solving method as long **division**. But because I am working with money amounts, I remember to put the **decimal point** in the **quotient**. The quotient is the answer.

When I use an algorithm, I set up a division problem. The number I am dividing is called the **dividend**. The number I'm dividing by is called the **divisor**.

$$2\overline{)3.50}$$

Then, I divide.

$$
\begin{array}{r}
1.75 \\
2\overline{)3.50} \\
-\,2 \\
\hline
15 \\
-\,14 \\
\hline
10 \\
-\quad 10 \\
\hline
0
\end{array}
$$

You may have a **remainder** when finding unit prices. In a dollar amount, quarters, nickels, dimes, and pennies have less value than dollars. And pennies, which are also called cents and represent hundredths of a dollar, have the least value of all.

So, if a quotient has three or more decimals, round the quotient to the nearest hundredth, or cent.

Is an algorithm a useful way to find a unit price? Why or why not?

Materials

- grocery store ads from the mail, newspapers, or online
- pencil
- paper

Coupon Collector

Have you ever shopped in or seen advertisements for a big-box store? If you were able to fly above a big-box store, you would see an enormous square or rectangular building. Inside are aisles and aisles of items, from gardening supplies to groceries.

Big-box stores buy large amounts of items so that they can sell them for less than smaller stores can. For example, you can buy a box of cereal that is twice the size of a regular box of cereal. And you can buy large **crates** of fruit instead of small boxes of fruit.

Look in your mailbox, in newspapers, or online for advertisements from a variety of food stores.

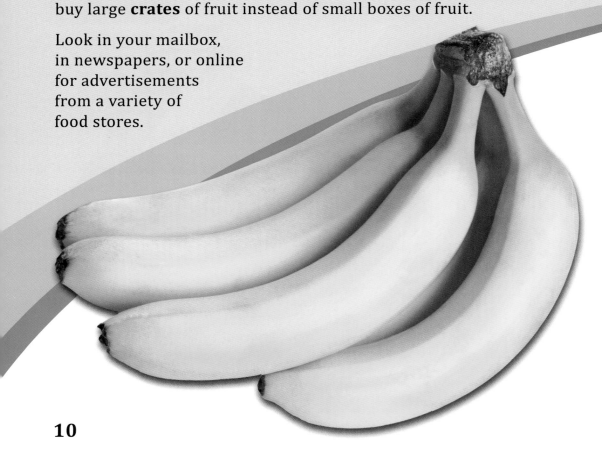

Find advertisements for the same product from two or more different stores. Record the price and the quantity of each product. For example, you might find bananas that sell for $2.29 for 2 pounds at one store and $1.02 per pound at another store.

Now, look at a package that contains more than one item, such as one package with four bars of soap inside. Divide the price of the package by the total units to get the price per unit.

Find as many advertisements for the same product as you can. Then, compare prices to determine where you can pay less for the same product.

Choose a method to find the unit prices. Or try several of them.

- use hundred grids
- use a double number line diagram
- use an algorithm

Breakfast Is Beautiful

Breakfast is Marty's favorite meal of the day. In fact, she'll eat breakfast at every meal! But her two favorite breakfast foods are cereal and yogurt. So, she compared prices of these two items.

Boing is her favorite cereal. *Boing* contains whole-wheat flakes and is loaded with chubby raisins. Marty always knows exactly where to find *Boing* in the store.

At our supermarket, one box of *Boing* sells for $4.00 and contains 16 servings. What is the unit price per serving to the nearest penny? Use a double number line diagram to find the answer.

Another supermarket in our town sells a different flake-and-raisin cereal called *Tiny Flakes*. The name should actually be Tiny Flakes and Raisins, because the raisins are really hard to find.

Anyway, the store sells *Tiny Flakes* in bulk, meaning in huge quantities. A 3-pound bag of *Tiny Flakes* is priced at $6.29. Remember that 1 pound is equal to 16 ounces. With that in mind, what is the unit price per one-ounce serving for a giant bag of *Tiny Flakes*? Try long division to find the answer.

Now compare the prices. That is, determine which costs less. Is it the box of *Boing*, or the giant bag of *Tiny Flakes*?

If Marty only ate cereal, breakfast would be a lot cheaper. But, she drowns her cereal in milk. Did you know that one cow produces about 6.5 gallons of milk per day? That's about 100 glasses of milk. Marty doesn't use that much milk on her cereal, but there are days when I think she comes close.

Marty's second most favorite food in the world is yogurt. Ordinarily, we buy yogurt in small containers. Each cup holds 3 ounces and costs $1.20. What is the unit price per ounce? Use hundred grids to find the answer.

 ## What's the Word?

Have you ever wondered where the word *yogurt* comes from? Or are you ever unsure how to spell it?

There are two standard spellings. One is *yogurt*, which is more common, and the other is *yoghurt*.

The word *yogurt* comes from an Old Turkish word meaning "to thicken." But how people first learned to make yogurt from milk is still a mystery.

One thing that Marty and I always agree on is that yogurt tastes better with fresh fruit in it. She really likes papaya, although I can't say it's my favorite. That is, it *wasn't* one of my favorites until I read a little more about it.

I was using the family computer to search for food coupons when I came across an article about payapas. "Marty," I said. "Look at this. People in Australia call the papaya a pawpaw. I think we should start using the same word, don't you?" She paid no attention.

The pawpaws we buy at Rob's Grocery come from Hawaii. On our last shopping trip, we paid $3.75 for 3 pounds of papayas. What is the unit price per pound?

Love That Juice!

Juice is at the top of *my* grocery list. My parents let me buy juice boxes because they are easy to pack for school. Sometimes, Marty drinks them, too. She likes the juice, and she likes that she can recycle the boxes. But I wonder whether there is a better buy.

At Rob's Grocery, we buy a brand called *Pour It Down*. It comes in packages of 10 boxes. Each box contains 6 fluid ounces of juice. The package usually costs $2.99.

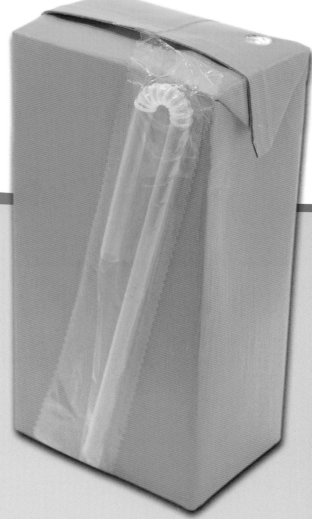

What is the unit price per ounce of juice in this package to the nearest penny?

We checked packaging and pricing at a different grocery store. The store doesn't carry *Pour It Down*, but it carries another brand that's almost as good. *Fruity Orchard* sells packages of 5 boxes for $1.89. Each box contains 6 fluid ounces of juice.

What is the unit price per ounce of juice to the nearest penny?

Now compare the unit prices. Which juice has the lower unit price, *Pour It Down* or *Fruity Orchard*?

 What's the Word?

The expression "cutting corners" comes from the days of horses and carriages. Drivers who stayed close to the corner when turning could save time. But they could also hit the corner and topple over. Today, the expression means to get fast results, even if it means risking safety. Businesses that cut corners use cheaper materials or pay less attention to quality in order to sell products faster and cheaper.

Popcorn!

We may not all agree on our favorite cereals or juices, but there's one food item we all insist on keeping on our grocery list. It's popcorn!

Marty and I snack on it between meals. And on family movie nights, Dad brings out our special popcorn pot. No one in our house watches movies without a bowl of popcorn nearby.

We often buy popcorn we can cook in a microwave oven. The *Pop-Magic* brand we like comes in a box of 10 bags. Each bag weighs 3 ounces, and the entire box usually costs $7.49.

What is the unit price per ounce of *Pop-Magic* popcorn to the nearest penny?

Of course, popcorn hasn't always come in microwaveable bags. When Grandpa was my age, his family cooked popcorn in a pot over a fire or on their gas stove.

Maybe, I think, we should check to see if buying popcorn kernels in bulk is cheaper than buying packages of *Pop-Magic*. Cooking might take longer, but I'm willing to make the sacrifice to save money. Who knows? Maybe I'll make extra popcorn and start selling it to my friends at school. That might be a faster way to earn money for a second computer.

We always have cooking oil and salt around the house, so to keep the math simpler, I'm not going to figure in those costs. I check the prices. I can buy a 2-pound bag of popcorn kernels for $2.98. So, since there are 16 ounces in a pound, that's 32 ounces in all.

What is the unit cost per ounce of bulk popcorn to the nearest penny?

Which kind of popcorn costs less, *Pop-Magic* or popcorn bought in bulk?

I had a great idea. It came to me because I couldn't stop thinking about popcorn. I could start a popcorn business. I could cook a fresh batch every night, bag it, and sell it the next day.

Maybe I could even spice it up a little. You know, add a chili spice mix to make it hot. Some people, I hear, like sweet popcorn. Maybe I could add sugar. Personally, I like cheese sprinkles on my popcorn, but Marty complains that it smells. I don't think I want to risk taking smelly cheese to school.

So, spice mix or sugar? Which will it be? I check some coupons to see what I can find out. Then, I check online. I never knew I could buy groceries online.

One online site sells herbs like False Unicorn Root and Frankincense Tears. How cool is that? But I'm not sure my friends would agree. I'd better keep it simple.

I can buy 5 pounds of a chili-powder blend for $53.00. Five pounds! That's a lot of chili! What is the unit price per pound?

Wow! I'm surprised at how expensive chili powder can be. I'm not sure how much I would use for every batch of popcorn, but it seems risky to spend so much when I'm not sure I can sell what I make. Maybe I'd better stick to plain salt.

I might be able to afford sugar. I check coupons and find a 5-pound bag of sugar for $7.19. What is the unit price to the nearest penny?

I asked Marty to do a taste test. I used some chili powder from an old bottle I find in a cabinet, and I took some sugar from the sugar bowl.

Marty tried the chili popcorn first. You should have seen her face. The words *grossed out* came to my mind first. Then, she tried the sugared popcorn. Again, more facial drama. I'm going to have to rethink my business plan. Until then, I guess it doesn't matter which one is cheaper.

If popcorn is important to me, it's not nearly as important as coffee is to my dad.

Dad seems to drink a lot of coffee. Well, maybe he doesn't drink a *lot* of it, really. After all, I'm not around during the day to watch him at work. But the coffee grinder wakes me up every morning. Dad grinds fresh beans and uses the ground coffee to make a pot of coffee. Then, he begins his work.

So, every week, coffee beans go on the grocery list. Dad has begun to look for a way to save money on his purchases.

The beans Dad usually picks out come in a bag of 32 ounces, which costs $24.99. What is the unit price per ounce of coffee beans?

Buying coffee in bulk might be cheaper. I like going with Dad to the bulk-food section. It's cool to lift the doors on the plastic bins and watch beans pour out the bottom.

Although all the coffee beans look pretty much the same to me, Dad says there are big differences in flavor. I am going to take his word on that.

Dad chose coffee beans that sold for $12.20 per pound. What is the unit price per ounce? Hint: Don't forget to change the pound to ounces before you calculate.

Which coffee is cheaper by the ounce, the packaged coffee or the coffee in bulk?

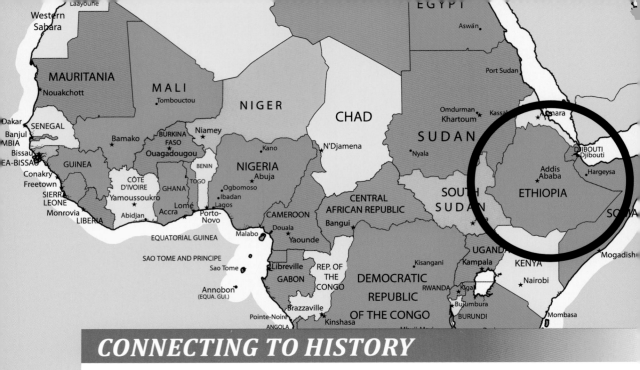

CONNECTING TO HISTORY

I did some reading about coffee online. There is a National Coffee Association that began in 1911. That makes it more than a century old. I guess coffee *has* been around awhile.

I linked to their history page and read about a goatherd named Kaldi. A goatherd is someone who herds goats. Kaldi lived in Ethiopia, a country in Africa.

The legend of Kaldi may not be true, but it's a great story. One day Kaldi watched his goats eating berries from a certain tree. That night, instead of sleeping peacefully, the goats were up and about, doing whatever goats do when they have a lot of energy.

Kaldi told the **abbot** at a nearby monastery about the goats' behavior. And about the berries. The abbot made a drink with some berries. The drink made the abbot more alert, even through the evening.

The abbot told a monk, who told a monk who told another monk. Soon, word spread beyond Ethiopia and reached the Arabian Peninsula.

24

Did you know that the word *café* is the French word for coffee?

The Arabs began to grow fields of coffee trees. They also began coffee trading. By the 1500s, there were coffee drinkers in Persia, Egypt, Syria, and Turkey.

The popularity of coffee grew, and soon public coffee houses opened across the Near East. People gathered to drink coffee, of course. But they also talked, listened to music, watched performers, and played games like chess. Coffee houses were lively. They were also places where people shared information.

European travelers to the Near East visited coffee shops and came home with tales of a new drink. By the 1600s, coffee was becoming popular in Europe. But not everyone in Europe was pleased. Some religious leaders wanted to forbid it. But before Pope Clement VIII ruled on the matter, he tasted the drink. He gave it a "thumbs-up," and the matter was settled.

In the Near East, coffee houses were called "Schools of the Wise" because people shared so much information while they drank coffee.

What Else Do We Need?

The item at the top of my mom's shopping list is rice. In fact, we *all* love it.

Have you ever thought about all of the different kinds of rice there are in the world? We're always trying something new. I choose brands based on their names. I think the names are fantastic! *Illabong. Kyeema. Irri. Hamim. Wagwag.* We buy *wagwag* rice grown in the Philippines. I checked the Internet to find the meaning of the word. It means "first class rice." I agree! It *is* first class.

At Rob's Grocery, a 5-pound bag of rice costs $20.45. What is the cost per pound?

Mom went online and found a bulk-supplier. We can order a 5-pound bag of rice for $14.15. Incredible! What's the unit price per pound?

Next, Mom examined the prices of the *really* big bags of rice that some supermarkets carry. We're talking 40- or even 80-pound bags of rice! My sister weighs about 80 pounds. But she's not for sale, of course.

A 40-pound bag of rice costs $15.99. What is the unit price per pound for this bag of rice to the nearest penny?

Which size has the lower unit price by pound?

Cluck, Cluck

Chicken is the most popular meat on our dinner table. As with most groceries, chicken parts come in different sized packages.

Meat prices seem to go up and down regularly. That makes labels even handier. The labels on packages of meat tell you the unit price. No calculations are required. The cost is usually per pound. So, heavier packages cost more. But, pound for pound, they can cost less.

For example, on our last trip to Rob's Grocery, a 2-pound package of chicken cost $6.64. A 5-pound package cost $15.30. What are the unit prices per pound for both of these packages?

No matter the cost, there's only one kind of chicken Mom and Dad are willing to buy. The meat has to come from free-range chickens. Free-range chickens don't spend their lives in cages. It costs more to raise them, so their meat costs more. But Mom and Dad say it's worth it. So, I'm guessing the chickens aren't going to help us buy a second computer.

Working in the Garden

Have I mentioned yet how much my dad loves broccoli? I can't explain it, but he does.

It isn't my favorite vegetable, but Dad reminds me often that it's good for me, and I don't really mind it. Especially if it's from my neighbor Amina's garden.

I work with Amina on her plot in the **community garden**. I help her plant and weed and harvest. She can grow broccoli for most of the year, but in winter, we have to rely on frozen broccoli. It's not the same, but thankfully, winter doesn't last long where I live.

Dad looked for broccoli in the frozen food section of Rob's Grocery. He found 1.5-pound packages for $1.92, and a 2-pound bag for $2.56. Which bag is cheaper per pound?

An Apple a Day

Finally, we have to talk about apples. Grandpa wouldn't last a day without an apple. You know the old saying, "An apple a day keeps the doctor away"? I don't know if it does or not, but it sure makes Grandpa happy. I am sure he would plant his own apple trees if they grew in pots on a patio. But they don't.

Grandpa could buy apples at Rob's Grocery, and he usually does when apples are out of season. But when farmers begin to sell fresh apples on the roadside, Grandpa visits every one of them.

Some farmers sell apples in $\frac{1}{2}$-peck bags. A peck is about 48 pounds of apples. How many pounds are in $\frac{1}{2}$ of a peck?

Grandpa bought 2 pounds of McIntosh apples from one farmer for $1.36. And he bought 3 pounds of Jonathan apples for $2.04. Which apples were less expensive per pound?

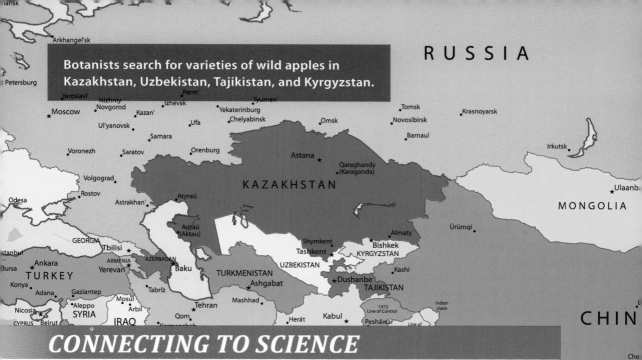

Botanists search for varieties of wild apples in Kazakhstan, Uzbekistan, Tajikistan, and Kyrgyzstan.

CONNECTING TO SCIENCE

Botanists believe the first wild apples grew in Kazakhstan. Today, botanists search there for new kinds of apples.

There may be several varieties of apples in your local supermarket, but they probably look similar. They are usually some shade of red or green. Wild apples can look "wildly" different. Some are as small as peas. Others are as large as small pumpkins. Even their colors are unusual. Imagine eating a cocoa brown apple.

Cold temperatures, the lack of water, disease, and insect pests can destroy apple crops. So, botanists search for wild apples that can survive these conditions. They want to use modern breeding techniques to create apples that are hardier and tastier.

An apple's genetic information is stored in its seeds. So, botanists at an orchard in Geneva, New York, freeze and store seeds in a seed bank. This has become even more important in modern times. As people develop the land where wild apples grow, wild apple trees are lost. A seed bank may mean the trees aren't lost forever.

MATH AT WORK

Supermarkets are common in many places around the world. They are entirely indoors, with long aisles and bright lights. Usually people enter the store, buy what they need, and then take it all home.

Farmers' markets are different. At farmers' markets, individual farmers sell produce they have grown themselves or other products they have made, such as jars of spices or pickled vegetables. Farmers need to know how to use math and unit prices when selling their products.

Open-air markets have been common since the development of agriculture approximately 5,000 years ago. A marketplace consisting of rows of stalls or shops was established in the

Sumerian city of Ur around 2000 B.C.E. The same kind of marketplace, called a *bazaar* or *souk*, is still common throughout northern Africa and the Middle East. People sell produce and other kinds of goods, from carpets to bowls to shoes. Sometimes an entire stall sells just spices and herbs!

In ancient Greece, a marketplace was called an *agora*. In addition to buying and selling food and other goods, the *agora* was a place for people to gather and exchange news.

Today, in farmers' markets around the world, farmers often display their produce on colorful blankets on the ground. In some areas of Vietnam and Thailand, people sell produce from boats, in a floating market.

Getting Supplies

We really have cut back on some of our family spending. Cable television is gone, and eating out is rare. And we use our library cards more often than we visit bookstores.

Mom takes leftovers to work for lunch. Marty uses less milk on her cereal. I pour juice from a bottle. And popcorn time is restricted to the weekends.

So, after only a few months, we decide it is time to think about what kind of computer we want and what kinds of extra things we'll need to go with it.

Sometimes, I need to use a computer at home and at school. This happens when I start a project at one location and need to finish it at the other. To do this, my English teacher lets us borrow flash drives, or memory sticks, for the year. I keep mine on my key ring.

My teacher searched online for flash drives in bulk. She found a site that sold 50 flash drives for $6.77. What was the cost per drive?

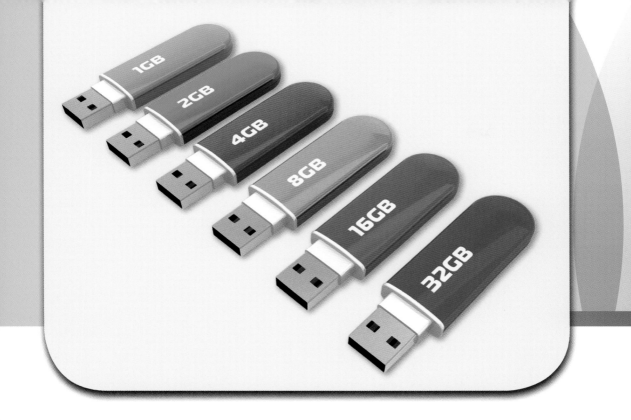

Different flash drives can hold different amounts of memory, or data. The amount they hold, expressed in units called bytes, is written on the packaging.

The prefix *kilo* represents 1,000, or 10^3 of a unit. A flash drive with one kilobyte (kB) of storage capacity can hold 10^3 bytes of data.

The prefix *mega* represents one million, or 10^6. So, a flash drive with 1 megabyte (MB) of storage capacity can hold 10^6 bytes of data.

The prefix *giga* represents 1 billion, or 10^9. A flash drive with 1 gigabyte (GB) of storage capacity can hold 10^9 bytes of data.

The flash drives my teacher bought hold 2 GB of data. My dad's flash drive holds 16 GB. I want one of my own that holds even more than that, but my dad says I'll never do enough homework to need it.

A Short Time to Go

"If we buy a desktop computer, we're going to need a new desk," I told my parents. "And a chair, too."

"I have a desk and chair in my room," said Grandpa. "You can put the new computer in there."

"Thanks for the offer, Pops," said Dad. "But there's an old desk in the attic. We can set it up in the living room."

"I love that old desk!" Marty said excitedly. "It has lots of drawers and a hidden compartment!"

"Marty, we're going to need some office supplies. Would you mind making a list?"

"Not at all," she said cheerily. She left the room creating a verbal shopping list. Sticky pads were on the list. She and I use a lot of sticky notes.

 **Did You Know?**

The Beginning of Sticky Notes

In 1968, Dr. Spencer Silver, who worked at the 3-M Company, created a new glue. The glue formed tiny balls no wider than a fiber of paper.

At the time, he saw no value for the glue. It wasn't strong enough for the kind of work the company was doing. So, no one thought about it for several years.

Then, in 1974, Art Fry, who also worked at the company, found he had a problem. He sang in a church choir. He used paper bookmarks to mark the songs the choir planned to sing at each service. But the bookmarks kept fluttering out and falling to the floor.

There was the problem. Now, Mr. Fry worked on a solution. He experimented with the glue Dr. Silver had created. The result was the sticky-note!

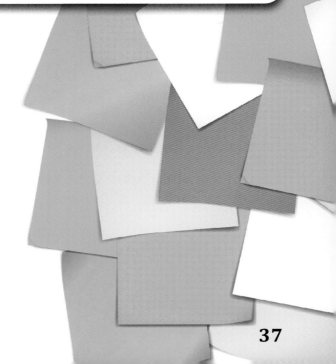

Marty found one package of 12 sticky-note pads for $17.50. She found another package of 10 sticky-notes for $14.00. What is the unit price of the 12-pad package? What is the unit price of the 10-pad package?

Which package costs less per unit price, the 12-pad or 10-pad package?

"Don't forget paper clips," I told Marty as she continued shopping online. "I like the colorful, jumbo ones."

"By the way, did you know that the first person to get a **patent** for paper clips came from Norway?" I asked. "He got the patent in Germany in 1899 and the American patent in 1901." I was feeling especially knowledgeable today.

"Do you carry a flash drive loaded with **trivia**?" Marty asked.

"Here's a package of 10 boxes of paper clips," she announced. "They're all one size, but look how colorful they are! The package costs $8.99."

"And here's another package of 12 boxes for $9.48."

What is the unit cost of the package of 10 boxes? What is the unit cost of the package of 12 boxes?

Which package costs less per unit price, the package of 10 boxes or the package of 12 boxes?

"Wow!" I said, looking at the computer monitor over Marty's shoulder. "Look at that wall of paper. We're going to need paper, you know."

Marty and I found rows and rows of **reams** of paper. "A ream is a certain amount of paper. Did you know that, Marty?"

"Yes, I did," she answered. "And did you know that a ream has either 480, 500, or 516 sheets of paper in it?"

My eyes opened wide. I had no idea how many pages of paper are in a ream. And I was surprised Marty did.

"The reams in these cartons all have 500 sheets of paper.

Here's a carton of 12 reams for $90.00 and a carton of 6 reams for $48.00."

What is the unit price of a ream in the smaller carton?

What is the unit price of a ream in the larger carton?

Which carton costs less per ream, the carton with 6 reams, or the carton with 12 reams?

The Savings Add Up

"We did it!" Mom announced one evening at the dinner table.

The rest of us stopped eating for just a moment. None of us could believe we had really done it! By using less and buying smarter, we saved enough money to buy a second computer!

For a moment, I thought Mom was going to start dancing. And all this time, I thought I was the one most excited about getting a new computer.

"What's the final amount?" Grandpa asked.

"We have $1,456.25!" she said happily. "We can buy a computer *and* everything else we need. Different kinds of paper. Personal flash drives. And desk supplies!"

"I think this Saturday is a shopping day, don't you?" Dad asked.

"Absolutely!" I yelled.

On Saturday, we entered an electronics store filled with shoppers. The store had every kind of computer and all of the gadgets that go with them.

There were phones, tablets, and televisions. There were printers, scanners, and cameras. And, of course, there were shelves of software, from office software to games.

There were aisles filled with office supplies, too. At first, I was a little overwhelmed by possibilities. But then I found the computer section. Wow!

We huddled around the computers, reading about and testing each one. We each chose our favorite computer and shared our reasons for buying it. In the end, we agreed upon buying a really cool computer for $999.00. It wasn't the least expensive computer, but we thought it was the best for us.

Dad used his calculator to figure out the tax on the computer. The tax added about $65.00 to the cost.

$999.00 + $65.00 = $1,064.00.

"Now let me solve a quick subtraction problem to see how much we have left over," Dad said.

$$
\begin{array}{r}
\$1,456.25 \\
-\ \$1,064.00 \\
\hline
\$392.25
\end{array}
$$

"Wow!" said Grandpa. "Can I have my own mousepad?"

We laughed. "You bet," I said. "And I know where they are. Let's compare prices."

"We'll leave that up to the two of you," Mom said, as she, Dad, and Marty headed to the software section.

We found lots of mouse pads in different colors. Grandpa suggested that we buy 5 different mouse pads for $1.95 each. But given our success in saving money, I suggested we check unit prices. I found a package of 5 black mouse pads for $9.00. How could Grandpa and I find the unit cost?

Idea 1: First, we could draw **hundred grids**. This method works well, but it takes a long time to draw enough hundred grids to show the total cost of the mouse pads. Plus, we'd have to buy some grid paper first, and we didn't want to do that.

Idea 2: We could make a **double number line diagram**. Grandpa likes using models to solve problems. But here we were in a store, surrounded by supplies, and we didn't have paper to draw on.

Idea 3: We could use an **algorithm** to find the answer. This is a quick way to find unit costs, although I always have to be careful to align numbers properly when I divide. Otherwise, it's really easy to make a big mistake.

"Let's use the algorithm," Grandpa suggested. "I found this old movie ticket stub in my pocket. It's small, but it's large enough to find the answer if we use an algorithm to solve the problem."

So, we let a tiny movie ticket stub make the decision for us.

"Okay," Grandpa said. "Let's think about the problem. The package contains five mouse pads. And it costs $9.00. So, we'll divide to find the unit cost."

"We'll start at the left and move to the right."

$$
\begin{array}{r}
1 \\
5\overline{)9.00} \\
-\ 5\downarrow \\
\hline
4\,0
\end{array}
$$

$$
\begin{array}{r}
1\,8 \\
5\overline{)9.00} \\
-\ 5 \\
\hline
4\,0 \\
-\ 4\,0 \\
\hline
0\,0
\end{array}
$$

$$
\begin{array}{r}
1.80 \\
5\overline{)9.00} \\
-\ 5 \\
\hline
4\,0 \\
-\ 4\,0 \\
\hline
0\,0 \\
-\quad 0 \\
\hline
0
\end{array}
$$

What was the unit price for the mouse pads in the package?

"Ahh," Grandpa said after the last step. "The mouse pads in the package are 15¢ cheaper than if we buy them individually. We could save money and put the savings toward a new computer just for me!"

"Sure, Grandpa. I'll buy you a new piggy bank so you can start saving right away," I said, leading him back to where the rest of our family was waiting.

How can you start saving? What will you save for?

To start, you need to know how much you can expect to earn in a period of time, such as a month. Perhaps you earn an allowance. Or maybe you mow lawns, babysit, or walk dogs.

Then, you need to know what you spend your money on. Keep a money diary for one month. You can keep a paper-and-pencil diary. Or you can use software to do the job. List everything you spend money on.

Then, in a separate column, write how much you spend on each item. Keep a running total. The results may begin to surprise you, even before you reach the end of the month.

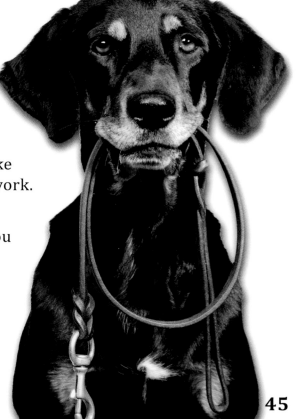

Now that you know what you earn and what you spend, you can think about how to save. Will you take your lunch to school? Will you buy school supplies in bulk? Make a plan of action. Then, put it to work.

Ask an adult to help you open a savings account at their bank. You may be surprised at how much you can save after only a few months. It may not be enough to buy a computer. But, you may be able to invite some friends to a movie.

GLOSSARY

abbot: the leader of a monastery of men.

algorithm: a step-by-step process for making a calculation.

botanist: a scientist who studies plants.

community garden: a shared public space in which individual people or groups each garden a plot of land.

crates: a wooden box with no lid used to ship fruits and vegetables.

decimal number: a number containing a decimal point.

decimal point: a dot separating a whole from the parts of a whole in a decimal number.

dividend: a quantity that is divided.

division: the operation of making equal groups.

divisor: the quantity into which another quantity is divided.

double number line diagram: a drawing of two number lines used to compare values.

hundred grid: a 10×10 pattern of square units.

intervals: a space between points on a number line.

patent: an official document that grants ownership for a product.

quotient: the answer that results from the division of numbers.

rate: a ratio that compares quantities measured in different units.

ratio: a comparison of two numbers or measures using the operation of division.

ream: a package of paper with 480, 500, or 516 sheets of paper in it.

remainder: the quantity left over after an equal number of groups are formed.

round: to write a number to a specific place value, based on the digit directly to the right of the desired place value.

strategies: a plan or method for solving a problem.

trivia: unimportant facts or details.

unit price: a ratio of a dollar amount to a unit amount, such as cost per ounce of cereal.

FURTHER READING

NONFICTION
Buying Goods and Services, by Lane Lawrence, Rosen Central, 2011
The Secret Life of Money: A Kid's Guide to Cash, by Kira Vermond, Owlkids Books, 2012
FICTION
Rock, Brock, and the Savings Shock, by Sheila Blair, Albert Whitman & Company, 2006

ADDITIONAL NOTES

The page references below provide answers to questions asked throughout the book. Questions whose answers will vary are not addressed.

Page 7: $1.75

Page 8: $1.75

Page 12: $0.25 or 25¢ per serving

Page 13: $0.13 or 13¢; *Tiny Flakes* cost less per ounce than *Boing.*

Page 14: $0.40 or 40¢ per ounce

Page 15: $1.25 per pound

Page 16: $0.05 or 5¢

Page 17: $0.06 or 6¢; Pour It Down

Page 18: $0.25 or 25¢

Page 19: $0.09 or 9¢; Popcorn bought in bulk costs less.

Page 20: $10.60; $1.44

Page 22: $0.78 or 78¢

Page 23: $0.76 or 76¢; Coffee bought in bulk costs less.

Page 26: $4.09

Page 27: $2.83; $0.40 or 40¢; The 40-pound bag costs less per pound than the 5-pound bag.

Page 28: $3.32 per pound for a 2-pound package; $3.06 per pound for a 5-pound package

Page 29: Both packages sell for $1.28 per pound.

Page 30: 24 pounds in $\frac{1}{2}$ peck; $0.68 per pound for McIntosh apples; $0.68 per pound for Jonathan apples. Both kinds of apples sell for the same unit price.

Page 34: $0.14 or 14¢

Page 37: The unit price of the 12-pad package is $1.46. The unit price of the 10-pad package is $1.40; The package of 10 costs less per pad.

Page 38: The unit price of the 10-box package is $0.90 or 90¢. The unit price of the 12-box package is $0.79, or 79¢. The package of 12 is cheaper per box than the package of 10 boxes.

Page 39: Each ream in the smaller carton costs $8.00. Each ream in the larger carton costs $7.50. The carton with 12 reams costs less per ream than the carton with 6 reams.

Page 44: $1.80

INDEX

CONTENT CONSULTANT

David T. Hughes

David is an experienced mathematics teacher, writer, presenter, and adviser. He serves as a consultant for the Partnership for Assessment of Readiness for College and Careers. David has also worked as the Senior Program Coordinator for the Charles A. Dana Center at The University of Texas at Austin and was an editor and contributor for the *Mathematics Standards in the Classroom* series.

Atlanta-Fulton Public Library